So they all rolled over
and one fell out.

There were seven in the bed and the little one said...

Roll over, roll over.

There were eight in the bed
and the little one said...

Roll over, roll over.

Roll Over

So they all rolled over
and one fell out.

There were six in the bed
and the little one said...

Roll over, roll over.

So they all rolled over
and one fell out.

There were five in the bed and the little one said...

"Roll over, roll over."

So they all rolled over
and one fell out.

There were four in the bed and the little one said...

Roll over, roll over.

So they all rolled over
and one fell out.

There were three in the bed
and the little one said...

Roll over, roll over.

So they all rolled over
and one fell out.

There were two in the bed and the little one said...

"Roll over, roll over."

So they all rolled over
and one fell out.

There was one in the bed and the little one said...

"Goodnight!"